AF346086

LILITH, the Enchantress

The evidence at the heart of the Myth

[A Universal Tale]

Eurydice REINERT CEND

Euryuniverse éditions

Legal deposit: January 2021

ISBN: 978-2-36331-141-2

EAN: 9782363311412

www.euryuniverse.net

DEDICATION

To Lilith.

To all the women, constantly and unjustly bruised.

To the women and men of good will who are always working so that all the creatures on earth can have a decent life.

To all those, children, men and women who are always and again suffering from the blind and sterile violence of those who seek joy only by imposing on others by force!

CONTENTS

Biography

Eurydice Reinert Cend was born in Benin in 1969.

She graduated from New York, U.S.A., where she stayed for 3 years and lives in France since 1991.

Holder of a DESS in Multimedia Communication and a Bachelor in Business Management, she has been writing since the age of fourteen and explores various literary genres including poetry, storytelling, novels and essays ... Eurydice Reinert Cend has published more than 35 books since 2005.

Author-speaker and journalist, she is also a member of the following cultural and non-profit organizations: ADILL, Sofia: Société des Auteurs Francophones and SACEM.

Eurydice was chosen as a member of the jury of the SNCF Foundation which goal is to fight against illiteracy from 2012 to 2014. She was also awarded the Naji Naaman international literary prize in 2015, in the poetic creativity category.

See the following websites for more information about her literary works and her press review:

http://euryuniverse.wix.com/euryuniverse

www.eurynews.com

www.euryuniverse.net

Facebook : Eurydice Reinert Cend

Bibliography

At Euryuniverse publishing:

- Lilith, l'enchanteresse : l'évidence au cœur du mythe, 2018

- Metamorphoses, collection of poems, 2017

- Baudelaire is dead, long live the poet, (opera libretto), 2017

- My truth, (testimony), 2016

- The Amazons of Knoryl, Vol.3 The Pact, 2016

- The Amazons of Knoryl, Vol.2 Remember, (novel), 2015

- The Amazons of Knoryl, Vol.1 The ritual escapade, (novel), 2014

- Under the baobab, listen: Tales and legends of Africa Vol.3, 2015

- Links of harmony (poems), 2014

- Under the baobab, listen: Tales and legends of Africa Vol.2, 2012

- Mom, like a sweet song, (collection of poems), 2012

- Why me? (novel), 2011

- Under the baobab, listen: Tales and Legends of Africa Vol.1, 2010

- The imperishable quest Vol.2: The heritage of Yohanan, (novel), 2010

- The imperishable quest Vol.1: Will you love   me? (novel), 2010

- The right to love, (novel), December 2008

-     Perfumes   of   Eternity,   (Poetry Collection), November 2007

- She, Ode to woman and to love, October 2007

- Let's not be afraid, (spiritual essay), October 2007

- Tales of today and everlasting time, November 2007

- Life in Poetry, (collection of poems for youth), November 2007, reissued in November 2009

- Rebirth in CHRIST, (testimony), 2006

- The songs of Eurydice, (collection of poetic songs), 2006

- The eye, (collection of poems), 2005

- Pépé Reinert, a visionary centenary, (biography), 2003

- The ABC of Love, for Her, (relational guide), November 2009

- The ABC of Love, for Him, (relational guide), November 2009

www.euryuniverse.net

www.eurynews.com

Thanks

Many THANKs to my family and friends for their truly warming support.

Cover image: an art work by the AI Dall-E

The author's word

If Lilith's legend was told you, would you accept it in truth, would you be willing to give up those certainties to which you were previously firmly attached? If Lilith was told you, yes, if you knew the strange truth that no one really dares to formulate with clarity, would you renounce to the stereotypes deeply printed inside of you? If so, and if you feel ready to venture off the beaten tracks and dare to discover her true story long garbled in the form of such a deplorable myth, then come and follow me on the wings of this tale, that is not really one.

Open the first page of this book if, and only if, you feel able to approach new shores, by no means familiar, with strength and courage! Lilith is your story and mine, beyond what has yet been said. She comes from far, far away, from so far away, we can't really say when. It goes back to the dawn of time to account for the possible existence of the man and the woman, the very first human beings created in the image of God by God, according to the holy text entitled Genesis.

Eurydice Reinert Cend

Foreword

"The Holy One, blessed be He," had created a first woman, but the man, seeing her rebellious, full of blood and secretions, had departed from her. So, the Holy One, blessed be He, has taken hold of her and created a second one for him. "- Yehuda Bar Rabbi (Genesis, Rabbah 18: 4), the Talmud.

Genesis is the first book of the Old Testament of the Christian holy Bible.

The character of Lilith, or Naama, is also known throughout the epic of Gilgamesh as an avatar of the Great Mother Goddess. We can also refer to the texts about this description of Lilith, etymologically derived from the phrase "Spirit of the Wind", the one that once fertilized, according to one of the beliefs associated with the legend of this rebellious woman.

The information about her has been meticulously eliminated from the biblical texts, to the exception of this passage of Isaiah (34; 14) which can be considered as a forgetting, finally proving in favour of this truth, deliberately obscured, about of the existence of the First Woman.

Lilith is well and truly recognized as the first woman in the ancient Hebrew legends, long before Eve, as well as through other mythological stories from around the world.

We are really appalled by the texts concerning the creation of the world, while reading the books related to her and stating the following reason, certainly judged to be inadmissible, explaining why she was so despised from the beginning: *she would have wanted to dominate the man, by putting herself above him during the sexual act.*

Crime of crimes. Such a terrible ignominy, so traumatic in the memory of the men of the first ages, that they resolved to destroy all traces of the assumed author of it: Lilith. This, probably in order to taint not the untouchable myth of man, almost always described as the dominant element of the couple. And, above all, to prevent Lilith from becoming, in any case, afterwards, a reference model for those of her condition.

According to the Talmud and to the Kabbalah of Judaism, Adam's true first wife, Lilith, was repudiated by him, then driven out of paradise by Yahweh, because she was rebellious to her husband and sexually unbridled, depending on the story that remained of her.

Demonized to excess, she would have been since then the concubine of demons in hell. Lilith would embody the female sexual appetite, as she is said to be the queen of succubus, the female demons that vampires the sexual energy of men during their sleep.

According to the Zohar, to the question:

"Who owns the child in case of separation? ", We find the following answer:

"On Adam's request, the Almighty sent three angels, Snwy, Snswy, and Smng, in search of Lilith. Finding her by the Red Sea, the angels threatened her: if she did not return to Adam, a hundred of her children would die each day. She refused, claiming that she had been expressly created to harm the newborns. However, she had to swear that every time she saw the image of these angels on an amulet, she would lose her power over the child. " And, until now, people of Jewish faith endow their newborns with amulets, whose function is to avoid this evil spell insidiously associated with Lilith.

Another later writing, Ben Sira's "Midrash", written around the 10th century, more explicitly describes the existence of this first woman. The name associated to her is that of Lilith, symbol of the rebellious woman, refusing submission and demanding a place equal to that of the man. Here is the content:

"When the Holy One, blessed be He, created the first lonely man, he said to himself," It is not good for a man to be alone. "He therefore created for her a woman taken from the earth like himself and He named her Lilith. From that moment, they did not cease to compete with each other. She said, "I will not sleep under you," and he said to her, "I will not sleep under you, but over you, for you are made to be under me." She then said to him, "We are both equal, since we both come from the earth." None of them listened to each other. Seeing this, Lilith pronounced the Wonderful Name and flew into the airspace. Adam stood in prayer before his Creator and said: "Sovereign of the world, the woman you gave me fled away from me". Immediately the Holy One, blessed be He, sent these three angels Sanoi, Sansano, Samnaglof, to go in search of her and bring her back. The Creator said to Adam, "If she wants to return to you, it's good, otherwise she will have to accept that one hundred of her children die each day." The angels left him and went looking for her. They surprised her in the heart of the sea, in the tumultuous waters which, in the future, will swallow up the Egyptians. They told her the word of the Lord but she refused to come back. They told her, "We are going to drown you in the sea." She replied the same thing already stated in the first version of this story, above. "

What else is to be said then to be conceived that all the judgments attributed God in the case between Lilith and Adam were so approximate, if not to say that they are absolutely unfair?

If we proceed to a rational analysis of the reported facts, the Creator endows Lilith with a pair of wings to allow her to flee away from Adam's presence, at first. Then, following the invocation of the latter, the God-Creator sends his angels to seek her to return to Adam, the same who wishes to force her to go against her true nature. However, when she refuses to submit to this request, the first woman is confined to Gehenna as a demon of the worst kind, as a child thief and as the persecutor of those. One hundred of her own children are condemned to die every day, in punishment for her insubordination, moreover ...! Is God still always good and merciful or not? If so, how can He allow one of His creatures to escape a situation that seems unfair to constrain her, firstly and a little time later, oblige her to accept the same fate she considers as highly unacceptable? There is therefore a strong contradiction between the true nature of the Divine and the facts attributed to Him. God does not contradict Himself, He does not perjure Himself and He cannot be at the origin of such bad, fundamentally unfair, incoherent and more than indecent judgments. Threatening with death, every day, one hundred of Lilith's children is in itself already an abominable thing, not to mention the constraint of returning to Adam which, this first woman thought so unbearable, that she preferred to endure the worst, rather than to submit herself to it. Decidedly, taken from every angle, the treatment inflicted on Lilith is nothing but foolish men's elucubrations, which cannot be associated with the supreme intelligence of God and, even less, with his magnanimity. All this is only a matter of man's precepts, from then and on, as Jesus of Nazareth reminds us more than once, especially through this passage from Matthew (19: 7-9), Holy Bible:

"Why then," said he, "did Moses command you to give the woman a letter of divorce and to divorce from her? He answered them, "Because of the hardness of your heart, Moses allowed you to divorce your wives; in the beginning it was not so. But I'm telling you that whoever divorces his wife, except for unfaithfulness, and who marries another, commits adultery. "

The heart of God is therefore much more lenient than the ones of those who have instituted laws, more than questionable, fundamentally in favour of their own interests. This, especially since the rules governing many human societies are clearly established at the expense of women's rights, considered to be inferior to men, for so long. Therefore, they often manage to shape the woman's mind in a lasting way, so, to obtain submission and obedience from her, as was required of Eve. Yes, Eve, this pure and admirable woman, who men seem to venerate so much, and who they very often hand over to the skies as a true woman model of reference. Eve, the eminent symbol of the submissive woman, the one who must always be dominated and controlled. It is therefore truly time to repair this terrible injustice perpetuated against Woman's bosom, out of sheer cowardice and convenience, for so many centuries. And this, supposedly in the name of God, by those who are so ignorant even of the real nature of the true gift of God which is, in essence, Love and Mercy, according to the holy books.

Finally, according to the Old Testament, did God not reveal his identity to Moses on Mount Sinai by proclaiming Himself: " I am The Lord, the Lord, merciful and benevolent God, slow to anger, full of fidelity and loyalty. "(Exodus 34: 6)?

And here is the first time of the biblical account of Genesis concerning the creation of the world as well as that of man and woman:

"Genesis 1

1.1

 In the beginning, God created the heavens and the earth.

1.2

The earth was formless and empty: darkness was on the surface of the abyss, and the Spirit of God was moving over the water.

1.3

God says, let there be light! And there was light.

1.4

God saw that the light was good; and God separated the light from the darkness.

1.5

God called the light day, and he called darkness night. So, there was one evening, and there was one morning: it was the first day.

1.6

God said, let there be an expanse between the waters, and let it separate the waters from the waters.

1.7

And God made the expanse, and separated the waters which are under the expanse from the waters which are over the expanse. And that was so.

1.8

God called the expanse above heaven. And there was an evening, and there was a morning, and it was the second day.

1.9

God said, Let the waters below the heaven be gathered together in one place, and let dryness appear. And that was so.

1.10

God called the dry earth, and called the heap of waters the seas. God saw that it was good.

1.11

Then God said, Let the earth produce verdure, grass bearing seed, fruit trees yielding fruit after their kind, and having their seed in them on the earth. And that was so.

1.12

The earth produced verdure, grass bearing seed after its kind, and trees yielding fruit and having in them their seed according to their kind. God saw that it was good.

1.13

And there was an evening, and there was a morning; it was the third day.

1.14

God said, let there be lights in the expanse of heaven, to separate the day from the night; that they are signs to mark times, days and years;

1.15

and that they serve as lights in the expanse of the sky, to light the earth. And that was so.

1.16

God made the two great lights, the greatest light to rule the day, and the smallest light to rule the night; he also made the stars.

1.17

God placed them in the expanse of the sky, to light the earth,

1.18

to preside over the day and the night, and to separate the light from the darkness. God saw that it was good.

1.19

And there was an evening, and there was a morning; it was the fourth day.

1.20

God said, Let the waters produce abundantly living creatures, and let birds fly on the earth to the expanse of the sky.

«1.21

God created the great fish and all the living animals that move, and the waters produced abundantly after their kind; he also created every winged bird after his kind. God saw that it was good.

1.22

God blessed them, saying, be fruitful, multiply, and fill the waters of the seas; and that birds multiply on the earth.

1.23

And there was an evening, and there was a morning; it was the fifth day.

1.24

God said, Let the earth produce living creatures after their kind, cattle, reptiles, and terrestrial animals, according to their kind. And that was so.

1.25

God made the animals of the earth after their kind, the cattle after his kind, and all the creeping things of the earth after their kind. God saw that it was good.

1.26

Then God said, let us make man in our image, according to our likeness, and let him rule over the fishes of the sea, the birds of the sky, the cattle, all the earth creatures, and all the creeping reptiles on the ground.

1.27

God created man in his image, he created them in the image of God, he created man and woman.

1.28

God blessed them, and God said to them, "Be fruitful, multiply, fill the earth, and subdue it; and rule over the fishes of the sea, the birds of the sky, and every animal that moves on the earth.

1.29

And God said, Behold, I give to you every herb bearing seed, which is on the face of all the earth, and every tree having in it the fruit of the tree, and bearing seed: it shall be your food.

1.30

And to every animal of the earth, to every bird of heaven, and to all that moves on the earth, having in it a breath of life, I give all green grass for food. And that was so.

1.31

God saw all that He had done, and behold, it was very good. And there was an evening, and there was a morning: it was the sixth day. "

Genesis 2

"2.1

Thus were the heavens and the earth completed, and all their host.

2.2

On the seventh day God finished his work, which he had done: and he rested on the seventh day from all the work, which he had made.

2.3

God blessed the seventh day, and sanctified it, because on that day he rested from all the work that he had created.

2.4

Here are the origins of the heavens and the earth, when they were created. ", (Genesis I & II: (1-4)) ", www.info-bible.org.

It shall be noted here that, only later, mention is made of the creation of Eve from a rib of Adam. In the following book: (Genesis II, 21-23). And that all that precedes this moment has always been carefully kept into silence, hidden to the possible. This is a further proof of the true desire to nullify the evidence of the existence of this disturbing first woman from the very beginning of these stories. As if the imagination of man could not conceive woman as a human being, apart from an obedient and servile creature!

Finally, through this tale, here is our own interpretation of what could have been the true mythical life of Lilith and Adam, in the first hours that saw the seeds of our fragile humanity in its first moments of stammering.

Lilith, the enchantress

At the dawn of time, in the dawn of all times, at the dawn of creation, in his great leniency, the eternal God decided to create the world. He separated the waters of above from the ones below and created the sky and the earth. The Creator ordered the waters below to gather in one place.

It was so, and the earth emerged from the space thus cleared. And God created the sun and the day, the moon and the night, and the lights over the firmament.

Then he commanded the creatures of the waters and those of the earth to appear and to proliferate after their kind, according to their nature, and so it was.

For five days, day after day, all this was created by Him. On the sixth day, the Demiurge wanted to complete his work with an extraordinary thing.

Yes, at the dawn of time, when the day still disputed the most beautiful part with the night and when the dawn was sometimes still mingled with the twilight, the Divine wanted to complete his creation by something that can always deeply move and question him. He created then the first couple of human beings. He created them man and woman, in his image.

The first man and the first woman were thus created at the same time, and not the woman from the man. He took clay, and modelled it into two distinct creatures that he wanted to complement one another.

When He was satisfied with His work, He breathed life into them and animated them by gratifying them with His breath. He told them who He was and why He created them. God instructed his creatures for a long time on what was essential for their well-being.

Then He blessed them, showed them paradise, and gave it to them, saying:

"Be fruitful, multiply, fill the earth, and subjugate it; dominate on the fish of the sea, on the birds of the sky and on any animal that moves on the earth. And God said, Behold, I give to you every herb bearing seed, and lying on the face of all the earth, and every tree having its own fruits bearing its own seeds: it shall be your food. Genesis (I, 28-29).

Yes, in the beginning, the first man and the first woman could eat all the fruits of all the earthly paradise trees, without exception. It will be otherwise only times afterwards, a long time after the course of events between these two human beings.

Later, yes, God will give life to another creature from a side of the first man, and not from one of his ribs, as is still said. But, in the beginning, yes, He created them: Lilith and Adamah, equally, without predominance of one over the other.

The first man was called Adama and the first woman, created at the same time as him, in the same way, from clay, the Divine named her Lilith.

Lilith was as alive as life, as beautiful as the bright day which, all, delights, as deep as the night that spreads over all her empire, without trembling, and as light as the wings of the wind that nothing weighs down. She was curious about everything and she used to enjoy everything.

Lilith liked to immerse herself into the heart of the Creation, she marvelled at it and delighted the Creation by her mere presence, as pleasing than invigorating.

Over the nights and days that passed, it seemed as if the life within Lilith was multiplying, as she joyfully fed on the life that freely abounded around her. The Divine Himself felt moved by her. And the Demiurge rejoiced for having created such a creature, in all, so admirable.

Lilith marvelled at the contact with the Nature as much as the Nature was delighted in the presence of Lilith. She irradiated the heart of the universe and the universe was rejoiced knowing that she was blooming inside of its heart, and God, himself, was proud of the fact that his creature was so wonderful.

As Lilith was filling herself with life and flourishing in the heart of the Nature, she also grew in intelligence and wisdom, and her jubilation sang Life as much as its wonders, sprung from the benevolent heart of the Creator.

At dawn, at the same time as the great star of fire rose, Lilith incensed and celebrated the Creation and, throughout it, life and the Lord who is the master of all. And the Demiurge rejoiced and felt so moved.

Adama, as much as he was concerned, contented himself with the fact of being part of the Creation, without really seeking to participate in its evolution. One would have said that he was satisfied with his fate and aspired to nothing else but the simple fact of belonging to the Whole coherent and, seemingly, sufficient part of life to him.

The man was getting up in the morning, giving thanks to the Demiurge, rejoicing himself at the sight of the fabulous paradise that surrounded him, as well as with the fruits overflowing, walking around, feeding himself and resting. Then, in the evening, he lay down next to Lilith, after having praised his Lord and God.

Like the plant that contents itself with being caressed by the invigorating rays of the sun, happily waving its branches at the gentle touch of the wind, Adama hardly questioned the true nature of the things or the depth of the mystery by which he was associated to life.

While Lilith, the first woman, was blossoming in the heart of the Creation, going from discovery to discovery, feeling blissful about everything she still wanted to know or loved to recognize, the first man contented himself to existing.

He preferred to settle down and to enjoy things nearby. He did not really seem to want to discover much more, beyond what was enough to maintain his livelihood. Adama dared not or did not wish to follow Lilith in the perpetual quest for novelties that inhabited her. Adama just enjoyed life, nothing more.

In the early days of their common existence, this posed not but a few problems. Each of them did as they pleased, then they met again, if necessary, to lighten together the immense loneliness that would have followed, otherwise. And everything was going well, at best, in the best of worlds.

On a fine day, Lilith came back to Adama after being away for half a day. With a happy expression and a dreamy air, she suddenly heard herself question:

- Lilith, oh Lilith, where have you been again? I've been here for hours, waiting for you.

- But, Adama, why wait for me so long? You know well enough that I never see time passing by during the day, since I'm having so much fun wandering here and there. And afterwards, I always come back to you, at bedtime, isn't it? So do not worry that much!

- I do not worry, I'm bored.

"Try to occupy yourself a little more, and you will not feel time passing by so heavily, Adama.

- To occupy time ...? I do not see myself running after butterflies, in vain, as you do, let alone, nor frolicking among water lilies.

- Oh, if only you knew the truth ..., I do not do just that! Well, today, for example, I let myself carried away in the butterfly round, as far as the morning breeze could lead them. And, after that, I listened to the wonderful symphony of the swallows, also joined by the ones of the turtledoves and of the blackbirds. Then, with an incredible delight, I went on the back of the zebra into the valley, where the big oak happily lolls. When we arrived, he swooned with pleasure and invited me to come and listen to his sweet heart's murmurs. That's what I have been doing for the rest of the time, being more than happy to discover a new life's mystery.

- You were listening to the heart of the great oak ...? And how did you achieve that?

- Just imagine that the beautiful giraffe of the meadows was passing by and that, helpful as usual, she made me climb on her back. I then sat on her neck and she put me on top of the giant tree. I slipped into the hallow of his branches, finding myself soon after all up on his trunk. And there, I had only to listen to his tender whispers flowing out and revealing such amazing things, that I remained absolutely amazed and thrilled for a moment.

- You listen to a tree that talks! But, Lilith, wake up now! Trees do not walk, do not speak and they don't have arms to embrace you as I do, I, Adama ...! yelled the man, at that time, with an incredulous air on his face.

"Adama, my dear Adama, if you were a little more curious about the true nature of things, you would know that the trees have thousands of feet, which lie beneath them, in the infinite depths of the earth, far away from the eyes. You would also learn that their branches, those innumerable arms of them, freely move, waved by the soft breath of the wind and happily sway themselves to offer a tender caress to whoever understands them, really.

"Woman, stop selling me your useless activity. I do not want to hear any more about all this more than sterile babbling.

At these words, no more procrastinating, Lilith joined the man, visibly upset. She slips herself into his arms, hoping to be able to ravish him from the dark mood that was raging by then inside of him. However, her heart was still truly hurt by the unthinkable disdain of her companion, who was only able to see things that reflected on the surface.

Nevertheless, the woman continued to pursue her existence according to her own nature. As Lilith filled herself with life and flourished in the heart of the Nature, yes, she really grew in intelligence and wisdom. And her jubilation incensed and praised Life and its wonders as much as the fabulous gifts of the Creator, everywhere she was.

By a bright and beautiful day whose course was already well underway, after spending fabulous moments in the Nature, Lilith crossed Adama who seemed to be desperately looking for her.

The hours of the day were already wildly falling, and the beings and the things were all preparing themselves to welcome the moon and her happy and more than fascinating procession of luminous stars.

Lilith had just spent a memorable day, started near the great spring, at the tumultuous waterfalls which often sang so happily.

Raised at dawn, almost at the same time as the blazing sun, she drank the morning dew above the sweet petals of flowers and gave thanks to the Creator, at the moment when the great star of the day plunged the Eden Garden into a flood of light with its soft rays, offering the view of a wonderful rain of light.

Rocked by the melodious songs of the fabulous paradise birds, Lilith crept into the scented spring, where thousands and thousands glittering and fascinating sun rays were bathing too.

After having rejoiced herself well enough, she came out even more eager to enjoy the countless wonders of the Eden Garden. The magnificent black thoroughbred on whom she loved to ride with great delight immediately offered her its silky back, in silence. Together, they rushed to attack the wide green valleys, hilly in places.

They even rode far beyond, melting themselves into the vast sandy expanse, opening at the feet of the mauve and blue mountains bordering the fantastic desert. Once there, they granted themselves a deserved break. Lilith then rejoiced with caress the beautiful mane of her majestic mount, which neighed then with pleasure for a long time.

She also plaited her splendid mount in places, and they laughed heartily, finding that very amusing. They moved then in the opposite direction, again, the woman and the beautiful mane of the fabulous steed whose braids were freely fluttering in the wind, exacerbating moreover the superb look of that royal animal.

They finally arrived at the edge of the great spring, when the horse suddenly suspended the beautiful momentum of his mad race and reared very abruptly, nonetheless, without dismounting its rider. They surprisingly saw Adama standing against the trunk of a willow, grumbling in his beard I do not know what unhappy word. Lilith, tenderly caressed the back of the thoroughbred, thanking him for being such a great companion. After that, she slipped to the ground and quickly joined Adama, suspecting the probable reason of the unhelpful mood he was showing, by then.

As she approached the place where he was waiting for her, even before she noticed that he was there, Adama could read on Lilith's face the drunkenness of life that characterized her whole person. And he was so jealous of that, thinking that he would never succeed in moving her as much as did the Nature in which she felt so happy, in the midst of the beings and the things.

However, Lilith had never criticized the man in any bad way. She was simply content to live as she intended to, while trying not to forget that he was also part of her life.

In spite of her thirst for discoveries and knowledge, she was always careful of his well-being, returning to join him more than once, during the day, in order to spend some time with him. Then, at night, she shared her bed with the man and fell asleep beside him.

But according to Adama that was not enough. The man always wanted more, as time passed by. He no longer veiled his disagreement about the freedom that his companion was so happily enjoying.

For all these reasons, Lilith finally moved slowly towards Adama, worried about what his reaction could be, for his mood did not suggest any good thing at that time. She ingenuously tried to slip herself into his arms, hoping to soothe his pain, someway.

Adama, however, repulsed her in a rude manner and went off, without a word, after having addressed her a bitter look, laden with a thousand of reproaches. If she tried to join him again in the moment, they would only argue in vain. Lilith stood there alone, then, sadly meditating on her fate.

The snake, as charming as ever, came and offered her one of its fabulous dances of which he had the secret, to help her preserve her joy. The birds were beautifully singing not far from her, delighting her with their so agreeable melodies. The wind joined the party as well, happily flicking the locks of Lilith's hair, whispering a thousand of magic things, efflorescing her skin in a clever and infinitely sweet caress.

Lilith was charmed by the benevolent nature of the beings and the things all around her. Hence, she went to meet Adama, only when she was at peace with herself again. That night, Lilith just lay down in silence, with her companion, sharing their common bed.

The next day, she awoke at dawn as always. After having praised the creation throughout the prayer offered to the Eternal God, at sunrise, Lilith went to gather tasty fruits that she brought back home and she shared them with the first man.

When Adama got up, she handed him a cup full of fruits, as irresistible as they were appetizing. Adama accepted this present without complaining, and he then reconciled with her, rather happy. After he had feasted, she kindly offered him:

- Adama, what if you were to come with me today to discover the things and places of paradise that you do not know yet ...?

"For what interest should I be running everywhere, up and down, as soon as I wake up? No, really, it does not tell me that much. I prefer to stay here and do things, the way I want to.

- If that is your goodwill, it suits me as well. I'll stay with you a little bit, and I'll leave after. However, I want you to be sure that I will surely be back before the star of the day is at the zenith.

- Go, Lilith, go. I am not holding you back.

Lilith went off to explore paradise, so, as she loved to do. She returned back home in time, as promised, careful not to abandon Adama ruminating alone, too long. They thus accommodated to each other, for some time longer.

None the less, the almost barefaced dissatisfaction of Adama brooded and grew up steadily, undermining as well any favourable ground of understanding between the first woman and him. He tried to contain himself for months, but it was in wasted effort. Each return of Lilith, which always appeared more than radiant, made him measure the emptiness of his own existence limited to the sole enjoyment of material goods.

On a beautiful day, rather bright and fresh, Lilith was returning from a fantastic flight on an eagle's back. The majestic bird had lent her the force of its wings to take her flying over the vast magical spaces of paradise. She had inebriated herself with the earthly beauties as much as with all the exhilarating sensations she felt during this magical flight.

Adama saw her descending from the back of the noble bird and he could only take umbrage of that, telling himself that his wife allowed herself all daring, obviously. The visible euphoria fully irradiating on Lilith's face added to the acrimony of the man. No longer able to stand that, he exploded with anger and immediately began to overwhelm her with rebukes:

- Lilith, here you are, at last ...! See which state you put me in. I've spent hours searching for you. And nowhere have I been able to find you until you reappear now, woman, as by magic.

- Adama, why are you still looking for me for so long?

- I miss you a little too much and I wanted you to be with me, as one, in the middle of the day. But, as always, you were not there.

- Could not that have waited for my return?

- No, Lilith, my desire of you is so strong that it is devouring me, as much as your absence insults me.

- You know that when I leave, it's often for a good time. Why, Adama, are you still striving to wait for me in such a desperate way instead of occupying your mind otherwise, until I come back to you?

"I do not have to occupy my mind with anything else but you, Lilith, if that is what I want. You are talking nonsense as usual. My mind commands me and I obey it. You should do the same, about me.

- Excuse me Adama, please, be clearer...!

- Yes, I order you, and you obey me.

- Big deal! Who do you think you're taking to, Adama? I agree to be your companion, but not your servant.

- Lilith, you owe me obedience, that's all. So, stop dithering and go to the evidence.

- And what's this evidence?

- I command, and you, you obey me without discussion! This is the indisputable evidence. The one and only one that is worthy to satisfy me.

- And where does it come from, your wonderful evidence, Adama?

- It comes from my imperious will and from the fact that the Creator certainly prefers it to be so.

- Oh? Really?

- Yes, Lilith. God wants us to be happy. But you alone seem to be absolutely rejoiced. For my joy to be complete, you must consent to obey me and to serve my will without questioning me always, woman ...!

- Do you forget that, man and woman, He created us, equally? Don't you no longer know that we both inherit of this paradise and that you cannot claim to be superior to me, as much as I cannot do to you?

- Stop justifying the unquestionable, that way, Lilith. If you obey me as I wish, we will both live happily, and I will feel less alone and helpless.

- And how should I obey you Adama?

- Lilith, listen! I want and I demand that you do not walk away from again me without my permission.

- Oh, Adama, my dear Adama, Should I wish it, that I could not do it. I would die of boredom, otherwise. Very often, at daybreak, I have already had time to do a thousand things before you wake up. And you want me to stay here, waiting for your awakening and till you to get up, to give me the right to go here or there?

- Exactly! You now perfectly understand me.

- Adama, even the animals and the plants are entitled to a better treatment. When all the Creation can pretend to be and to enjoy a fair freedom, you, my companion, you would like to deprive me of mine?

- Lilith, I do not wish to deprive you of your freedom to be, but only to coordinate it with mine. Thus, shall we live in great harmony and will we be happy together!

- I am really sorry, Adama. So sorry for not being able to abound in your direction. Your need for harmony is the opposite of mine and I see no reason to submit myself to it.

- Not only will you submit to it, but shall you begin by immediately satisfying my desire of you. Woman, lie down here under me, and let me rejoice myself of you, so to appease the torments you keep raising in me, constantly.

- Me, to lie there, under you, just because you order it as a master ...? Adama, aren't you dreaming!

- By fair means or foul, Lilith, you'll have to obey me, he threatened the woman again, approaching her abruptly, with the aim to physically submit her to him.

He then tried to topple her under him in order to satisfy his seething desire. But the woman, as fat as a feline, and no less strong than her companion, physically, swiftly escaped from the grip of the latter. In her turn, she darted a thundering look on him, while throwing him these bitter words:

"Who do you think you are, Adama? Do you really think that you can submit me to your will just because you want to? Submit yourself to your own mind as much as you pleased, but do not ever try to impose on me in any way and, even less, by force.

- Lilith, listen to me! Lilith, obey me and stop arguing with me that way, all the time. I want you to stay with me instead of running here and there, whatever the weathers. See, the animals, all the beings as well as all the things enjoy your presence more than I can claim to. You are my wife, you are mine. Stay with me and do as I ask you, that is all I want from you. Lilith, listen to me! he said again, trying to convince her at the end in a supplicating way which was betrayed nonetheless by his threatening gaze.

- But Adama, don't you see that we have the eternity for us. What would it be like to live while continually staying in each other's presence, as you wish so much? I think we need to space our moments of reunion, somewhat, in order to better appreciate life together, over time. Otherwise, boredom would easily take over and we will quickly feel annoyed by each other, don't you think?

- But I'm already bored, Lilith. I miss you always and, your continual absences, they do not help...

- I assure you, Adama, that you'd better to be bored of my absences, rather than be irritated in my presence, because my person finally weighs you down.

- Here you are again with your great speeches. Quite procrastinating ...!

Woman, notice that from now on, I will no longer listen to your nonsense nor let you impose on me so freely, as you are used to. You have to obey me, and that's all ... "exclaimed Adama, at the summum of exasperation, his eyes raging with such a vivid and unbearable anger.

- I am just trying to tell you things as simply as I understand them, Adama. I do not impose anything on you, just as you should not seek to submit me to your will, regardless of my freedom to be. Try to be less demanding, less authoritarian and, perhaps, will we come to an acceptable agreement, you and I.

- As it seems that strength is not enough to bring you to do what I want, for the last time, Lilith, lie under me as a sign of obedience, otherwise, I will call for the God Creator, and He will severely punish you.

- Do that, Adama. Just do that...! I will never stay under you as a sign of submission. Now, Adama, listen carefully to this: Lilith obeys only to Lilith and to her Creator, the Lord and

Master of all. Lilith obeys only to Lilith and to the Lord, her Creator and God she repeated, adding:

- If I had let you come over me, sometimes in the past, it was only with the will to play with you along with the desire to satisfy you. But then, you were not so pretentious and, even less, so proud. From now on, you have lost that privilege which only belongs to my own free will. If it cannot tolerate me as I am, your pleasure will no longer be nourished at the expense of mine, in the future. Do you understand well enough what I'm telling you right now, Adama?

- Well, I understand that you're still refusing to obey me. If that is your desire, woman, let it be so! I'll promptly act to guarantee mine. I do not want you anymore in my life, Lilith. You are only a pure source of nuisance to me, and I want you to know it. I refuse to continue to suffer your presence, which is really not profitable to me, ideally.

At these words, Lilith withdrew from the cave that served them as home. While leaving, the woman cast a look, strongly marked with spite, to the one who had been created at the same time as her, equally, and in the same way, but who was standing then insolently in front of her, claiming some supposed rights, he thought he held over her.

She pronounced the wonderful and secret name of God, afterwards, and immediately she found herself in another shelter. Henceforth, the first woman lay far from the wrath of Adama, inevitably unleashed against her person in those times. She could not understand why he could attack her with so much fury, going so far as to wish that she disappears from sight, forever.

The man had become as another. She wasn't able to recognize him, many times ago. He often complained against her and rarely had soothing words for her, except when he wanted to mate with her.

Seeing that Lilith flourished in contact with nature much more than in his presence, while he felt invariably satisfied with his condition and the natural order of things, the man began to take umbrage.

Little by little, his mood went from discontent to rage. Adama realized, oh yes, how much this creature, brought to life at the same time as him, surpassed him in all respects. He also understood how much the Nature and the Creator rejoiced in the presence of the woman. The one that seemed to shade him, the man, much more than she finally amused him, according to his own thoughts.

Lilith revealed herself as the majestic jewel of the Creator, the materialized vow of the universe, and Adama became aware of this, day after day. The more the evidence imposed itself to his heart, the more it irritated him, and the more Adama turned his heart away from the one of his wife, into the wonderful paradise they had inherited of, equally.

In reality, the Creator who knows everything well wanted to allow them to take the necessary time to calm down, hoping that they would be able to reconcile without his intervention. But, seeing that neither the woman nor the man showed the slightest desire to reach out to each other, in order to make peace, he finally acceded to Adama's request, manifesting himself to him throughout words.

From the beginning of the ill-being that gripped Adama, the Demiurge, to whom nothing escapes, saw the man being consumed by bitterness and jealousy. And that greatly desolated him. And He feared the worst for these two wonderful beings He created in His image and whose existence had been eagerly desired by His loving heart.

But He did not want to intervene, leaving them free to decide what course they would like to give to their lives. One had chosen to fill herself with life, while the other was content to solely belong to life. The demiurge respected their respective choices, realizing how the two creatures He brought to life, in the same way, could evolve in such opposite ways.

He feared the final outcome of the acrimony that was eating the man's heart away, hoping that he would be able to temper his moods in order to regain his inner peace and to strive towards a purpose that would bring along good.

This would have been clearly acting in favour of the woman and would have emphasize the admirable side of her nature in comparison with that of the man, if He had expressed Himself earlier, to decide between them. But God could not disavow one of his creatures, without disavowing Himself. He wanted them to freely decide for themselves and to strive towards the destiny of their choices. To act directly in this case would have been to force Adama to realize the fact that he was misleading himself and that he was mistaking seeing Lilith as an enemy.

Adama could, as much as Lilith, use his mental abilities to invest himself in the quest of the Creation' wonders. But he just did not want to do that, or maybe had he not realized that it could be of some use to him to live another way. The Creator was rather saddened by this situation for which Adama called to Him, at the height of confusion. Seven days later, He manifested himself to the man:

"Adama, my beloved son, you have invoked me, here I am. What can I do for you?

- Great Lord, thank you for answering me so quickly. Here is my problem. I can no longer stand the woman you gave me for companion and, I would like You to let me separate from her forever, if possible.

- To repudiate Lilith forever? And why this, son?

- She is unbearable and always acts as she wants to. I find myself alone so often, and this situation distresses me and it's terribly weighty to bear, day after day.

- Is this the only reason why you want to banish Lilith from your life?

- Not happy to abandon me whenever she wants to, she refuses to lie under me, furthermore...!

"Adama, my dear child, do you only know what you are asking me now?

- Yes, my Lord and God, the woman never wants to obey me and I feel more than upset by her attitude, which constantly oppresses and hurts me.

Please, bring her back to the right path or make her disappear from my life forever, I beg You. Otherwise, I do not know if I will be able to continue living that way.

Of course, the Creator was more than saddened by the resolution then taken by Adama. He was even more so when he saw how much the man whom he had created himself hated the woman born at the same time as himself and in the same way.

God heard the terrible request of Adama by then, and said to Himself that He had to act without further delay. He decided so, having thoroughly probed Adama's heart and found that the bitterness inside him was such that no reasonable advice could diminish it. He was filled with great compassion for each one of His creatures, however. Hence, He decided:

- Since this is your own will, I will bring away from you and for ever, Lilith, the woman created at the same time as you. Having said so, God called the woman and commanded:

- Lilith, come on, let's go!

"Here I am," replied the woman, who had appeared at once, at the request of her creator.

- I'm ready, Lord, let's go.

- I cannot stand her anymore. I don't want to see her ever again, exclaimed Adama, still full of wrath, when he saw Lilith for the last time!

The Creator removed Lilith from the paradise where she had been born and where she loved to be so much, satisfying thus Adama's request to the possible extent.

But, as she left, one last time, Lilith turned back to her former companion and threw him these words in a murky but firm voice:

"Man, never call my name again, anywhere, for it has become impure in your mouth. You are unworthy of it, henceforth, and it will be only sacrilege if you dare to name me again, as you know...!

Adama turned away from her abruptly, unable to endure the intense gaze of the one who had just imposed her own limits to him, in the end. He quickly veiled his face with his hands then, as if he had been struck by an invisible sting.

Hence, the man would never forget the expression of immense sadness then shading the wonderful face of Lilith, of which he could not stand neither the sight nor the brightness anymore. He was forever marked at that time, as if the too bright glow of an unbearable light had just hurt his eyes, when they met the ones of the woman for the last time.

The Divine then haloed Lilith with his breath to shield her from Adama's eyes, who could not help but turn one last time to see her go away from him, forever. The man saw Lilith fly into the air to disappear from his life, from his world, till the end of times. Her cloths floating in the wind, within the clouds, surrounded her with a subtle screen of mystery that he, the man, could never pierce nor penetrate.

The last image he could grasp of her was that of her bruised face turned to him and questioning in silence him with a memorable and poignant: " WHY? "

Undoubtedly, the serpent was there, from the beginning of the life of Lilith and Adama. Like all the animals, the trees, and the other landscape elements, he was fascinated by Lilith and used to follow her, wherever she went. The snake was never far away from Lilith. He saw everything and heard everything that was said between the man and the woman, then.

And, when Lilith was forced to go away from the original paradise, the serpent was the first to be overwhelmed among all the beings that belong to the Creation. And he was languishing, and he was so angry about the man. With all the others, the beings or the things belonging to the Creation, he lamented about Lilith's banishment from their world and the inevitable boredom that would follow, with no doubt.

Lilith was the flame of the Creation, the one by which paradise was able to reborn to itself and was renewed through the luminous and fertile gaze of the one who knew so well how to receive from it and to give herself back to it in a total and fully uncommon way. The whole universe was therefore sad along with the world, and the stars were veiled by the shadow of the dark confusion hence engendered. And God deeply questioned Himself at that time about the uncertain future of his Work, as He did about the true nature towards which the beings, He created in his image, would ultimately tend to.

Lilith was languishing in the place where God had installed her, while He was still trying to find a solution to Adama's case.

She wondered why the Creator had so quickly satisfied Adama, perhaps disavowing her in the mind of the first-man. What was her true place in the Demiurge's heart? Did she have the same rights as the man?

What exactly was the Creator expecting from her and would she really be able to meet His expectations? For Lilith, one thing was by then sure and crystal-clear: « she would never submit herself to the imposing arrogance and to the more than flagrant will of domination of the man. » As much as she was concerned, it would be better to have never been born to life rather than to live and suffer such a deplorable fate.

Lilith already knew then what it's like to suffer. At present, the anxieties of the uncertain future came to sum up with the rest, shading moreover her future's horizon, seemingly more than nebulous, from now on.

"The God Creator must love Adama more than He appreciates me. Otherwise, how to explain his quick decision in favour of the man and this silence towards me? That's how Lilith was sadly lamenting, alone in the landscape devoid of life and with a lunar atmosphere in which she finally found herself. Her reflection inevitably oscillating between defective trust and insidious doubt:

"How can one understand that the Lord has so promptly abounded in the sense of Adama, without having heard me? Really, I do not understand that and I find it deeply unfair. Unless there is another explanation that still escapes to my mind, I do not know if I will be able to continue to rejoice as one of the Divine's creatures anymore. What have I so badly done to become so unworthy in the eyes of Adama and, perhaps, also in the sight of the Lord? I was rejoicing myself so much, just by the feeling of truly belonging to the world of which I have just been banished, now. I did nothing but to live, loving life and exalting each one of its wealths. Is that enough to hate me and punish me so cruelly?

Adama would have certainly wanted me to be more present by his side! But how could I have endured living in his own way, only, without the feeling that I was continually sacrificing myself thus, by the time? I have only obeyed to my deep intrinsic nature, the one which has always pushed me to want to meet the beings and the things, my own way.

Doing this, always, with the desire to grasp the true beauty and the real essence of each of them. No matter how hard I tried, I could not bear to stay inactive for a long time in Adama's company, without feeling truly tortured. Not to be free to move at one's ease, isn't it the same as no to exist at all, in short? To be living, is that still worthy, if one must always be restrained without being able to respond to one's own aspirations? To love another one, is it in the end a good reason to compel him or her to continually act contrarily to his or to her own nature and will? Adama reproached me to have not loved him enough. However, had he only loved me just a little bit for having behaved in such an ignoble way, as he did with me?

For if so, would he not have tried to understand me a little bit, instead of trying to force me to exist only according to his own selfish desires? No, this life is not really worth living, if it only boils down to exist according to the sole will and wishes of someone else. When the Creator comes to me, I will confess my displeasure and ask Him to make me go back to the nothingness from where he pulled me out, rather than to let me pursue such a pitiful existence, I will never accept. The birds freely spread their wings wherever they're pleased to. Even the plants are free to let their branches swing in the wind. And I, endowed with a Master, the greatest of all, who created me in his own image, I could not enjoy the same freedom...? To be said truly, I am awaiting to know the outcome that my Lord and God is planning for me before I resolve myself to the worst. I still hope in His good heart, even though the recent events have plunged my heart and mind into such dismay", was Lilith then wondering.

God came back to Lilith much earlier than she expected. He murmured softly in her direction, so as not to frighten her, while she was still meditating on what her fate would be. He knew that she was tormented by what happened and was also aware of the inner debate that was going on in her heart. But the woman immediately turned away from the Creator and threw herself face down on the ground, as a sign of submission and respect, as soon as she noticed His presence.

- Lilith, my beloved daughter, what are you doing...?

- I'm veiling my face in the eyes of my Lord and God because I strongly displeased You, as it seems, and I can no longer plunge my eyes into Yours.

- What are you saying, child? You did not displease me at all. I've waited to come to find you, but I did not forget you. Lilith, my joy, my marvellous flower, don't ever again doubt my love for you! Now, stand up and come to me. Dry your tears and rejoice, Lilith, my child.

- Ô great Lord, my God, do you not want to punish me for the blame that Adama overwhelms me with?

- No, my dear daughter. You displeased only Adama and I do not seek to punish you.

- May I rise then in dignity ...?

- Certainly, my daughter. Don't you know that you are, so far, one of the most beautiful jewels of my Creation? Lilith, my dear child, you are the splendour which rejoices my heart, when I see you living just marvellously according to your own nature.

- You do not blame me then, Lord, for having offended the man, as he claims?

- By no means! Each one of you shall choose the destiny that best suits him or her. Adama has just chosen his and you are also entitled to the one you deserve.

- I now dare to cling to hope again, my Lord and God.

- Now, yes, dry your tears and rejoice again, knowing that I love you at least as much as Adam.

- Here I am, rather reassured, my great Lord and God. Full and infinite gratitude, always, for your great leniency as well as for your admirable justice.

You are my daughter, Lilith, never forget it.

- What will happen to me Now, Lord?

- I let you meditate on the exchange we've just had and I will come back soon to reveal what I expect from you. We will discuss it together, and you will tell me if you do agree with it.

When God returned to Lilith sometime later, they firstly talked about Adama, because the creator saw that Lilith's heart was still troubled by the discord between the man and her.

- Lilith, my beloved daughter, pour out your heart and truly free yourself from what is still cluttering your mind. My joy cannot be restored as long as one of the finest flowers of my Creation will remain so altered.

- My Lord, I still do not understand why the man condemned me and hated in this bad and sad way. Why that ...?

- He allowed himself to become envenomed by jealousy, that is why he dislikes you so much.

- What is jealousy?

- That is what a being feels, when he or she is envious and wants to have the things in possession of another, or what he or she seems to have more than does the jealous one, according to the latter. It is an evil feeling that gradually gnaws at the heart of those in whom it infiltrates itself, and it is a vice that end up destroying them, if they persist in feeding it.

"But I possess nothing more than Adama, Father!

- Probably not, but he does not know that. In fact, you are at the best of your abilities and of your mental skills, much more than he is, and he's very angry at you, actually, for that reason.

"Adama is angry at me for that ... but why is he not doing the same, since he is as well able to do so?

- Simply because of his lack of will. It is this same defect that makes him prefer to overwhelm you, rather than questioning what can be changed or improved about his own nature.

- Can we thus change nature?

- But of course, Lilith. You are evolutionary beings, for the best as well as for the worse. I would prefer for my part that you could evolve into good. However, it is up to you to freely choose the path that you want, during your existence, according to your heart.

- Being that Adam blames me for his own weaknesses, that's one thing. But why did he want to condemn me to disappear from his existence in such a cruel way? Am I such an abominable creature? Am I not alike him?

- Certainly, yes. Each of you develops different addictions, though. The man, I've created at the same time as you, loves to bask in the paradise, while you enjoy rejoicing as much as investing yourself into it. He does not like loneliness, but he also refuses to act in such a way as to break that feeling, as long as it costs him. The only solution he has found in this case is, seemingly, the one of putting the blame on another and, therefore, on you! Yes, Lilith, the man could blame no one else but you, since you, alone, appear to be equal to him, in truth, in addition to the fact that you were so often living in the presence of each other.

- To reject the fault on me, is it all the man found fair to do about me!

- Lilith, my daughter, this is not fair at all, of course, and it has a very special name.

- Which one? What's the name given to such an injustice, Ô Great Lord?

- It is called treachery or treason, and this phenomenon is certainly born from cowardice and lies.

- Lies…!

"Yes, by refusing to consider his own mistake, Adama is lying to himself, pretending that you are unworthy of him for reasons which only suit him, alone, and which are so far away from the truth.

- Why refuse to share with me the so vast and big enough paradise, able to welcome thousands and thousands of creatures, in this case?

- Out of pure jealousy, Lilith. Lie is born out of jealousy, which produces nothing good. Seeing you flourish, day after day, while enjoying a stable existence less rewarding than yours, nevertheless, Adama fed an unhealthy desire inside of himself.

- Why does he envy me that much, since he has freely chosen to live as he pleases?

"Because you stand for what he cannot be, due to his real lack of good will, and because he prefers to hate you, rather than to admit this sad truth which is so much unbearable for him, sadly.

- I had to disappear, hence, so that Adama will no longer undergo the comparison, isn't it?

- That is right, Lilith. Your presence had become a perpetual torment for your companion. The shame he felt because of his own inability to take care of himself had gradually transmuted into bitterness. Then bitterness has become hatred, and this terrible rancour has led to your blame.

- I understand this terrible situation better more. From now on, can I at least continue the course of my life, in peace, although all this is already engraved in the deepest of my being, and even if it will probably always be so.

God blessed Lilith afterwards, and He then placed her on a very beautiful planet of which she remains the only mistress, ever since.

While still waiting for God's decision, Adam walks in a paradise where all the creatures and the things are now laughing at him, accusing him of being responsible for Lilith's unfair fate.

The sun now veils himself with shadow, over the passage of the man. He has called upon the darkest clouds to wrap the horizon with the colours of sadness, only, every time Adam emerges from his refuge to show up within the nature.

- She is no longer here, Lilith, the luminous, the true splendour of the Creation in the presence of whom I was so eager and pleased to fertilize the world. She is no more here, the resplendent flower of the Divine, once offered to the contemplation of our eyes. Why should I keep bathing this pitiful world with my sweet life-giving rays, when the only one able of the true hearty generosity is no longer the mistress in this sad and desolated paradise I am still supposed to regenerate, day after day, tell me? No, for the moment, I'd better hide myself, rather than pretending to rejoice for the achievement of such a thankless task. Without Lilith, who really deserves now the invigorating warmth I freely offer here...?

"And what about us, ô, beautiful star of the world, so dull in these nebulous days? We, too, are sad to die for not being able to enjoy anymore the sweet and beneficent presence of Lilith, exclaim the others in chorus, immediately afterwards. And the lion roars in the direction of the man with a ferocious air, for the first time, threatening him with his terrifying fangs, while questioning him:

"Man, why haven't you taken pity on us if not for yourself? Why did you overwhelm the woman, furthermore, willing to disown her in the eyes of the Creator? She is no longer here, the one who used to pass her beautiful and sweet hands in my waving mane to make me purr with pleasure and bless the Demiurge of the grace thus offered to me. With who could I gallantly walk in the wide wild world, henceforth, happy and proud to be fully recognized for who I am, truly speaking? Who will murmur into my ears these mysterious words that only Lilith knew well how to formulate and pronounce. No, really, Hurry to get away from my sight. Order your steps to quickly carry your body out of my presence before I lose patience ... *RRRRRRRRRRRRRRRR*, roars again the majestic feline.

The snake starts whistling as Adama approaches, becoming more and more aggressive, in turn, casting at him a look of reproach, more than elusive.

The whole forest remains silent, as soon as the man dares to enter inside of it. The trees hastily order the wind to move away from them for a while. The birds immediately suspend their melodious songs. The turtledove plays the dead, so as not to have to look at the man.

As Adama moves away from the forest, overwhelmed by the rebellion of the beings and the things that belong to his world, the raven circles around him, transforming his once wonderful song into a long and, more than unbearable, impertinent croaking.

They all clearly recriminate against the man, while exalting the nostalgia of Lilith's presence, whom they miss so much ... "If only Lilith were here ...", has then become the continual chorus by which they all persist to overwhelm the Adama, from then on.

The monkey, who once kindly mocked the man and the woman, making them laugh to the point at wringing guts, now cheerfully laughs at Adama. He gives him more than contemptuous grimaces, insolently sneers against him, then he turns away from the man, and nothing more, when he dares to approach him.

The moon has suddenly gorged herself with red and black colours, in an unnatural way, as if willing to symbolize the nature of the tragedy by which the world is suddenly deprived of its most prodigious pearl. She has turned into a kind of black moon, imposing such overwhelming laments on Adama, that they turn out to be poignant to the rest of the Creation.

The dawn, meanwhile, sighs and complains a lot:

- Adama, O Adama, why are you not the last of the living creatures on Earth! From now on, yes, who will come to embrace me, at the same time as the star of the day, to feast on my thus exalted splendour... who, tell me who?

And the wind, after him, begins to grow.

- Oh, poor, poor me! Who will now lend me her beautiful waving hair so that I let my invisible fingers run in with a pleasure beyond measure? Who, tell me who? Then, addressing the others, all around:

- Yes, who tell me who? And when, in turn, the twilight makes its more than noticeable entry, he exclaims upon his arrival, in a very distressed and upset way:

- And, here I appear, without anyone to welcome me nor greet or thank me. Once, Lilith would have offered me her wondering eyes so that I could dive my soft reflections in, at leisure. Oh, here I am now, more than cursed ...! Oh, where is our Lilith, where is she now...?

- Shut up! Shut it up, all of you! She isn't here anymore, your Lilith. There is no more Lilith here. Silence ...! yells Adama, suddenly overcome by the whole Creation, which seems to have turned into an interminable lament against him, by then.

In their turn, the lion, the panther and the tiger began to roar, as much as the wind, once again, becoming really bad. Altogether, with the others, they tirelessly repeat and repeat this terrible chant, which only incriminates Adama forever and again:

"No more Lilith, no more Lilith, no Lilith, how sad, how sad ...!"

Inconsolable and unable to reduce her pain, the magpie starts to harass Adama with questions, very loudly, in a piercing voice:

- Why did you let Lilith go, Adama? Why, why Adama, why ...? didn't she stop repeating, until Adama finally answered, in a full of despair and wrath tone:

"You all know that Lilith was not really mine, she has never been mine, anyway!

"But she loved you, Lilith, more than anyone and more than anything else," the bird exclaims.

- She loved me more than anything? No, I do not believe that! She was always everywhere, except with me.

- Adama, oh Adama, stop doing the child as much, by now! Lilith joined you every night; the woman spent a good part of her days with you, and you, you are now standing there, complaining because she did not share every single moment of her life with you ...!

- That's not quite the case. In reality, each of you enjoyed her presence much more than I did...! Now, leave me alone with your whining. Lilith is no longer here, and that's better, "concludes Adama in a bitter and irrevocable voice. The bird then flies away, leaving the place to drown his sorrow far away in the blue of the horizon, much more tinted with shadow than light, in these desolate days, when the sun was given of itself to the Creation with great reserve. Adama then begins to move away from all of them, forcing the pace, while becoming indignant through this long monologue he served:

- Enough, I have more than enough of your incessant recriminations against me! What is it that she possesses more than I do, your Lilith, so that all of you are ceaselessly mourning like this, because she is no longer here ...? Let me hear that! Lilith, your Lilith, is no longer of this world and, I alone remain the human creature of God that you will have to accommodate with in the future. You are suffering so much, ha! And, still, what about me? Do you think you really know what suffering is? But where were you while your so beautiful Lilith was disobeying me, ignoring me and doing things only the way she liked? Oh, yes, I remember now! But, yes, she was always with you, among you, sharing everything with you ...! And, you would now like me to repent for what I have received from her, which is still a gift, so far, less than did the smallest of you? No, no and no! Your justice is not mine and I will never consent to submit to the moods of a female! I am fed up, tired of all of you! Do you hear me...? Now, silence ..., still erupts Adama, fulminating, and almost at the threshold of madness, before he concludes:

- Do you really think you are more worthy than I in the Divine's heart? I do not believe so. Only Lilith's madness kept her away from me, so often, giving you preference. And, that, I would not tolerate any more, just as I will no longer support your endless taunts. The breath of God lives in me, truly. As a result, you owe me obedience and respect, all of you! Is it clear enough...? ", the man shouts again, visibly at the height of dismay.

Seeing that, the Creator intervened once more in his favour. Since He had placed the human being above all other creatures, at the time of Creation, God could not go against His own word.

The Divine returned to earth after three days, since the man was now so despised by the Creation, to His great regret. Then He commanded all the animals and the things to act according to the peaceful feature of their own nature and no longer according to the aggressiveness they were also able of. The Demiurge went away afterwards, having promised Adama to return to him on the seventh day.

At the time of the promised encounter, God proposed Adama to choose a wife according to his own desires.

- Adama, my son, I gave you a first companion. But obviously, she was not acting the way you wanted her to. Now, truly tell me, how do you see the one who could ideally share your existence?

- Lord, I see myself in the company of a kind, gentle and, above all, not always upsetting woman.

- Is it really only a docile and loving companion that you want, Adama?

- Yes, Lord. I do not want to find myself anymore in the presence of a woman who always contradicts me, giving me reasons to torment, more than necessary. What I want is a woman who is the complete opposite of the first one.

- All the opposite, really?

- Would you like her ugly and always silent, instead, son?

- Certainly, not. However, I would like her to be speaking only to please me, and not trying to discuss my orders, all the time.

- If I give you such a wife, Adama, are you sure you will be able to cherish and treat her as well as should be?

"I am sure of that, great Lord. In truth, it is a woman of this vein that I really need.

- If you do not act according to your promise, the consequences will be disastrous, are you only aware of that?

- I take the risk, and I will do my best to respect my wishes.

- Know that, from now on, the fruit of the tree of life will be forbidden to you, to your new wife as well as to all those your lineage. So that to preserve your vow, once realized, you can no longer eat it under any pretext, from this day on. Otherwise, the order of things, as you wish, will irredeemably be broken and you will only have to suffer from that, then.

- Let it be so, Lord. Paradise is full of delicious fruit trees and the one of the trees of life will not be missed. If this is the only sacrifice, I must make to have a woman in conformity with my own wishes, I willingly consent to it.

"It will then be done according to your will, my son. However, try to keep your promise and make sure that your wife is faithful to you, still recommends the Demiurge.

But Adama did not yet understand the true significance of these ultimate warnings formulated by the Creator.

"Since I am the only man who can rejoice of her presence, how could the woman be unfaithful to me, not to mention the fact that she will easily obey me ...? No, I do not risk anything about that, "he told himself then, minimizing the last words of the Devine.

Having heard the man's requests, God realized that only a submissive woman would fulfil his expectations. So, he acceded to his demand, hoping to please him thus, while preserving harmony on Earth.

However, Adama did ask the Creator about what would happen to Lilith, without naming her, in accordance with the prohibition imposed on him by the first woman. He inquired of her to the sole purpose of making sure she was not better off than him. The demiurge quickly swept the space in front of him and showed him where the woman was, still waiting for Him to drive her to the ultimate place planned for her.

It was then a nebulous environment, without any other living soul. But that perfectly matched Lilith's mood and her needs for meditation at the moment. However, the Demiurge said nothing of this to Adama, who hastened to think that the woman, rejected by him, was relegated to hell in the end. And the man will teach his people later on with this same hasty conclusion, more than false.

After that, God called a deep sleep to fall on Adama, who fell asleep and He pulled the woman he truly wanted from one of his sides and, not from one of his ribs, as will be said later on. In doing so, the Demiurge hoped that the man could not blame the creature born from himself, drawn from his own substance, afterwards. He already anticipated the possible causes of discord between them, in the future, knowing that this would not prevent the man from acting only according to his own interests, if he so decided.

Upon awakening, Adama discovered Eva, who was lying nearby him.

"Here is the flesh of my flesh. This one is my wife! The one who obeys me and will love me as I want. Together, we will be happy ", he exclaimed, gazing at her, amazed by this discovery, feeling more than content.

"So, let it be, and remember your promise, Adama. Cherish the woman as much as possible. Love her as for yourself. Be happy, be fruitful, and dominate all that lives above the earth and in the waters. If you break your vow, the consequences will be terrible and I cannot decently remedy.

Then God showed them the tree of life and truth, from which they could no longer eat fruit, henceforth, if they didn't want to suffer the more than regrettable consequences that would follow. God reminded them again of the prohibition that was linked to it, because of the change introduced in the initial order of things by the will of the man.

Indeed, the man and the woman could no longer eat the fruit of this tree, since Adama's deep desire was to ignore knowledge, while keeping his companion in the same state of mind as his.

That's how is born the myth of the forbidden fruit, which was not before, at the time of Lilith's presence on earth.

From then on, eating the forbidden fruit would bring back the man and the woman to a new state of consciousness, which would annihilate irretrievably the one finally custom-made by the Creator to Adama. Only disorder and disorder would ensue, inevitably, with their unavoidable cohorts of vices and evils.

Afterwards, Adama and Eva lived long happily. In accordance with his wishes, Eva never questioned Adama in vain, did not insist much on his refusals, and did not even think of rebelling.

However, over time, the repetitive life of the so desired woman began to weigh her, as was to be expected. As did Lilith before her, Adama's new companion began to ask herself questions about the true essence of things, though she did not try to explore the Nature in order to impregnate herself with it.

Eva did not talk much with Adama about her subjects of reflection, fearing to displease him, otherwise. The snake that almost always followed her, as he did with Lilith, quickly understood what was going on in her mind. He saw her becoming more and more sad when she was, at times, alone.

Nevertheless, as soon as Adam was with her, she recomposed herself quite a happy expression, in order to avoid arousing suspicion in him, and not willing to break the *beautiful* harmony so much favoured by her companion.

The serpent was truly ravished inside, carefully waiting for his hour. He had then only one desire: to take revenge on Adama. To make fun of him because of whom Lilith was no longer present in paradise.

Eva gave birth to several boys in the early days of her motherhood. As long as they were still children, innocent and helpless, Adama was amazed. But as soon as they began to grow in strength, their father complained and became jealous, fearing a future rivalry between them and him.

Adama could not bear the attention filled with infinite tenderness with which Eva cared for her sons. He was so jealous and suspicious that he finally became terrifying. He often chased them from home, as soon as they reached the height of an adult man, in order to prevent any form of conflict between them and him, later on. The father wanted to make sure that he would always be the only one to enjoy his wife's affection.

Eva had a growing fear for the fragile safety of her children. She feared that their father would do them irreparable violence. So, one day, after Adama had entered into a frightful anger, accusing her of adultery with one of his banished sons, Eva took refuge in the shade of the tree of knowledge. She sat at the foot of the sacred plant, meditating on her fate and on the behaviour to be observed in order to escape the growing and more than outrageous suspicions from Adama.

The snake, which was never far away from the woman, slowly approached then and made sure to catch her attention. He began playing hide-and-seek with Eva in the foliage of the sacred tree. And, as inadvertently, he dropped one of its fruits. Eva arose immediately and wanted to move away from it, remembering the Creator's formal prohibition about it. But the snake shouted at her in his hissing and cajoling voice, saying:

- Woman, here is the solution to all your problems. Eat of this fruit and you will never again have to fear the terrible vexations to which Adama continually submits you. Here it is, taste it now and see life and the things of the world, as they really are.

- Snake, but you're crazy! Aren't you? What an idea to only want to disobey the supreme will of the Creator ...! exclaimed Eva suddenly, absolutely terrified and trembling.

- No, you're wrong! By eating this fruit, you will only disobey Adama. Are you not overwhelmed by seeing yourself continually so ordered and demeaned in the eyes of your own descendants?

- You can trust me. Eat this fruit and you will be a better woman, and Adama will respect you much more! he then added, noticing that she remained petrified and silent.

- I will be a better companion and I will win the respect of Adama, if the snake is right. So, maybe will he stop suspecting me of adultery as well as blaming our children in vain..., said Eva to herself, finally, while moving away from the tree.

Eva saw Lilith in a dream, the following night. Lilith was so beautiful but also so sad! She was so sorry for the fate that was overwhelming Eve, in her turn. The first woman whined about her sister of fate, deploring the perverse nature by which the man she had once known was such a regrettable selfish husband, thinking only about his own desires and satisfaction. "Listen to me, Eva. I've already been through these same paths you're now walking in. I'm so sorry to see that you are enduring all this… ", she told her. Eva bitterly cried in her sleep, finally realizing that her companion would never stop doubting about her and hurting their children, in the sole purpose of preserving his own privileges.

Once she woke up, she was already different. The expression of her gaze had changed. Her once tender, though, sad eyes now seemed to be resolved as well as drowned in spite. Melancholy and distress had dug deep furrows into her, from which tumultuous waves of bitterness finally sprang. For the first time in her life, Eva greeted Adama without looking into his eyes. She served him the usual cup of fruits and the scented water which he delighted himself of, at the first meal of the day, just after having done his ablutions. Then, she briskly and quickly went away from their hearth.

At the foot of the tree of knowledge, the snake was already present, waiting for her. He said nothing at first, as her whole person was betraying the woman's despair, which was also visible in all her gestures and expressions. The reptile contented himself with playing in her presence, without trying to disturb the madness' dance of the dark emotions which was taking place in her mind. Eva came nearby and stayed not far from the tree. Then, indecisive, she went several times around it.

But after a while, unable to contain the rage that threatened to explode with anger inside of her, if she did not react quickly, she finally went to the tree of life with a determined air and picked one of its fruits. Eva waved it to her lips and ate it hastily, before regretting her gesture and before she would have to give up. The snake came closer to her, then gently wrapped himself around her body, and he finally congratulated her for her great courage.

"Daughter of the earth, from now on, here you are, mistress of your own destiny!", he declared with a knowing air. Eva remained with him in silence for a moment, the time to realize the full extent of the act, hitherto inconceivable, she had just completed, however. Eva had just braved the main prohibition emanating from the God Creator, indeed. She discovered herself in a new way, immediately after, to her great astonishment. For the first time in her life, she was ashamed to see herself all naked. So, she hastened to cover her body with large leaves held together by a green cord.

Back at home, Eva began to hide away from Adama's eyes. She dared not answer him then because she was absolutely petrified by remorse. She naturally wondered what would be the man's reaction, not forgetting the one from the Creator. Nevertheless, Adama quickly realized that the nature of things had irreversibly changed, for the worse. He then meticulously watched his companion and saw that she was dressed with green sheets and asked her the reason why.

- Adama, we cannot continue to live like this, anyway. Don't you see that we are all naked?

- Eva, of course I see that. We are naked, so what? What is now so embarrassing about that?

- Look, even the animals are covered with hairs, while we are as naked as worms.

- So, what, Eva? That did not bother you more than that, before. Why put yourself in such a state of mind because of your nakedness now?

- Because I can't stand it anymore.

- What did you do, Eva? Tell me the truth. I find you suddenly so changed ... What's really going on here?

Eva suddenly turned away from her companion and remained silent for a moment. Then she turned back to him again, with a guilty look, saying:

- Anyway, you would have ended up knowing the truth. So, here it is, I ate of the sacred tree's fruit.

- How dare you, Eva ...! We are done. What will the Lord say and what will become of us now? Do you only realize the disaster you have just engendered?

- It's too late, I'm sorry, but I needed to know.

- But to know what ...? You're crazy, I can swear! To know, to know…, here we are, badly done because of you, woman!

- Not so badly done, maybe not. Since I have eaten of the forbidden fruit, I can see the world with a new eye.

- And this new eye, what does it teach you better than you didn't already know, woman…?

- It tells me that before me, in your life, there was this other woman named Lilith, for example.

At these words, Adama became pale at once. He realized that he had no other choice now, but to know about the true nature of things too, at least as much as his own wife, from now on. So, he rushed at the foot of the tree of life, in turn, and ate of its fruit, after screaming his rage at the face of Eva, now disenchanted and more than disturbed by all this.

- Never say that name again in my presence, woman. Let no one pronounce that cursed name in front of me, in the future, either. I forbid you to do so, the children as well, because it is unworthy and does not remind me of anything good. This woman was only a vile demon, do you hear me, Eva? Yes, a demon of the worst kind ...!

Adama refrained from pointing out that it was Lilith, herself, who had forbidden

him to pronounce her name in the future,
since he had stood up against her as an
absolute and total enemy.

In the beginning, Eva had been able to raise a boy after another to the time they reached adulthood, until the birth of her first daughter. Adama loved this child so much that he took her for a wife, as soon as she was old enough to share his bed as such. Very busy in satisfying his more than beloved daughter, he abandoned her mother, his rightful wife, and took much less care of the fate of his sons, fortunately for them.

Adama had many sons from Eva, before. At first, he marvelled at becoming father, but he hated them soon enough as they grew up and filled their mother's heart with great joy. The man killed some of them, also, before they were strong enough to be able to fight him.

Later on, he wanted to attack one of his male children again, but his other boys interposed between their brother and their father, threatening the latter physically. They forbade him from harming any of them in the future, under penalty of reprisals. Adama had to obey them from now on, because he had lost the great physical capacity that allowed him to force them to obey him by force, in the past.

Adama had also established his own law on his offspring and briefly mentioned the name of the first female creature of God, only to blame her and to reduce her to the image of an infamous demon. He pointed out the immense horror he still felt for Lilith and proclaimed that the example of this vile creature should never be followed. According to him, it was God Himself who would have turned this evil woman into a demon, because of her devilish nature. Whoever imitates her would be reduced to the same state, hence, since then.

From the reproach surrounding this terrible prohibition, which now has the force of law, was born the sacrilege surrounding the memory of Lilith, the first created woman, since the dawn of time. Her name, as well as her life, has become taboo, since then. Rites of purification were even initiated to ward off the evil supposedly associated with her person. This, in accordance with the despicable prescriptions of those who legitimated the abominable lie against her in an insipid and more than infamous truth. These rituals are still taking place today among the communities who inherited from this distorted legend, along with all of the prejudice related to it.

Lilith actually inherited of an ethereal universe with a peaceful and purplish atmosphere. Fantastic creatures evolve in joy and peace there. Their mission is to continually exalt Lilith's taste for life. Unicorns, fairies, elves, dragons ... but also other amazing creatures, by her chosen from the terrestrial ones she loved so much, can be seen at this place. On her new planet, Lithos, Lilith preferred the dragon to the snake and, the serpent will always be angry at her, for this same reason.

The extent of Lilith's power has been revealed to her by God Himself. She can move from one universe to another by the force of her sole will, for instance.

God offered her, moreover, a universe where everything is light and proceeds from splendour, inspiring harmony and pleasure to the beings who live within it. Then He created a companion to the expectations of the first woman. This wonderful being, Lilith named him Erosethos. Then the Demiurge asked Lilith to bring to life herself, with her own breath, the one who will be, and who has been since then, her ideal double.

However, Lilith will never reveal this to her companion, whom she has wanted her equal, nonetheless, and the one she has always considered as such, since these immemorial times. Erosethos is at the height of her expectations, for her greatest joy. He is evolving since then as the quite perfect complement of the first woman, and not as a rival.

In a universe far away from that of Adama, the world of the Lilithians and life on Lithos have nothing to do with the despisable hell to which Lilith is supposed to have been condemned, for eternity. The first woman reigns in her own realm as a being of Light. Lilith is not the vile creature, rejoicing herself throughout evil and finding her justification only in absolute horror, as is still said nowadays.

Adama's world is the one inherited by the mankind of those who are still living on earth, today. It is the one where women are always still begging men just with the hope to be able to live in peace, with dignity. This world has been perverted since then, unfortunately, as it only expresses itself under the evil seal of Adama's rules. Adama, the first traitor engendered by the universe. The one who betrayed Eva, as well as he had already betrayed Lilith. Poor man, never happy! According to him, if the woman, such a miserable and unworthy creature, had not pleased him because she was rebellious and infamous, she had certainly obliged him to disobey the Creator! Woman, the absolute evil conceived by the first man's mind, only, according to his own aspirations for shameful perversion.

We can then understand, as well, the reason why women are still that much persecuted, today. The shameful reason why they have so much difficulty in making themselves heard and in obtaining the legitimate respect owed to them, even by those they give birth to, hence.

Nonetheless, among the men and the women who inherited of Adama's world, some are able to develop skills similar to those of the Lilithians. Perhaps, are they from Lilith's offspring or of the lineage of those who, sometimes, come from the first created woman's world ...? May be are they those extraordinary beings filled with compassion and truly eager to love their neighbours as much as for themselves! Those rare and so inspiring people who come to show the way to their peers on earth, from time to time.

Aren't they, perhaps, the so-called Manasseh, Melchizedek, Orpheus, Jesus of Nazareth, Krishna, Zoroaster, Buddha, Mahatma Gandhi, Martin Luther King, Mother Thérèsa, Nelson Mandela, Michael Jackson ...? Those who have always been able to privilege the truly positive human being's values to vanity and selfishness mostly related to the will to possess?

We are always been told that Lilith would have become a demon, since she was separated from Adama. That she would still be wandering now in hell.

But I do not believe that. Demon, but why demon, actually? Demon for having refused to obey Adama? Demon for having rebelled against the purely sterile, perverse and selfish will of her first companion? No, I really do not believe that.

To attribute such a shameful crime to God, isn't it to insult the great intelligence of the Divine? Actually, who is the creature able of an infinite and rare intelligence that would reduce the most precious of his creatures to the ignoble and deplorable state supposedly reserved to Lilith by the Creator, in the end? And, this, always according to the distorted version of her legend, a more than unnatural history transmitted by the men of the first times, who were so busy to silence the terrible and so disturbing truth about Lilith and Adama? Isn't God still God, the Almighty and Merciful Lord then, to be reduced to such an absurdity, to an aberration of the most blatant, besides the more than infamous aspect of this judgment? A decision as iniquitous as devoid of common sense, moreover.

Dear readers, here you are now, in possession of the most objective version, to this day, of this universal legend about the origin of the existence of the first woman and man, created by God. It is now up to you to evaluate its most likely nature according to whether you wish, or not, to move away from received ideas, to tend towards this plausible truth, herein, suggested.

Best regards,

ERCEND, Eurydice Reinert CEND

Songs and laments

The first tear of sadness

The first tear of sadness

Which wounded the heart of the universe

It came from Lilith, the high priestess

By God wanted as equal to the first man,

Wounded under heaven's skies,

Since then, stained.

She faced the very first world's lies

And since then, every wound engraved

In the ravaged heart of every human being

Every tear that springs from the haggard gaze

Of those who daily fear for their future

Paved with the capricious paths of destiny,

Echoes this initial distress

Which saw the clouds whining and light veiling itself

And by which the first paradise had been altered, since!

The first tear of sadness

That sprung from the eyes of the High Priestess

Still finds its echo today

In all the cries of anxiety

Of all those who are overwhelmed by so many evils

That they keep dragging and carrying such heavy burdens

On their human and so frail shoulders

All those who are flooded with so many zeros,

Poor lost heroes!

Lilith, the enchantress

Here is the dawn, so wonderful and bright

The blue, the white and the gold colours are all blazing in the sky

Under thousands and thousands of the sublime sun's rays

The Green world from its light break, slowly, awakens

Fountains, rivers, and seas

Are all still languishing in their imperceptible sleep

And here she is, sublime and light,

Overflowing the whole Nature

Of this very grace that fertilizes and liberates

The star of the day, showing up with his majestic crown' halo,

All dressed in a veil of mystic light!

And, together, the amazing Lilith and
the mythical Sun

Drink, enchant and shape

The Creation throughout their true acts
of devotion,

Enchanting the Whole, giving thanks to
the Divine

By this sublime osmosis

Which, all, metamorphoses,

In the majestic and invigorating moment
of their unalterable symbiosis!

Then, the whole Nature with them feasts
and, again,

Dares to drink at the source of Life

In the name of the Master of all things.

Praise and praise, you all, in the joy that
all engenders!

Lilith, the enchantress, and the original
sun,

Altogether, make this heard everywhere

Joy, joy, peace and joy, always and again

Joy, joy, peace and joy, that's our only
true treasure!

Where is my place now?

Into this very great paradise

I no longer feel in heaven

Joy is leaving, hope is falling

As love betrays and dies

And looking around, oh

I see nothing remaining of us, no
ooooooooooo

So, where is my place now?

Where am I supposed to be,

Ooooooooooooooooo oh

Once all has been lost with the fall

Leaving me nothing more

Than this terrible wall

Now erected between you and I, all
apart?

The sea whispers to my ears

With the wind soughing all day long

The sun sheds down its purest rays

With the clouds dancing in the best way

The earth asks the falls, the volcanoes and all the springs

To dance and sing along with all that owes wings

My soul is still sad and inconsolable

As my tears dried out,

And, here I stand, alone and voiceless

In the front of the curse calling for madness.

Why, Adama, why?

Why Adama why?

Why did you throw all the joy to dust

And kill the flame and trust

We once shared with devotion and love?

Why Adama why?

Why did you kill innocence

Leaving now place to this blatant offense?

Why Adama why?

Why have you lost faith

And decided to burn hope

Then breaking love's amazing rope?

Why Adama why

Why should we lose paradise

While we were meant to shine

So pure and brilliant in the magnificent
sunrise?

Why Adama why

Why are we now enemies

While we once drowned into bliss?

Why Adama why?

Oh, tell me why

You have left doubt, lies and jealousy

Win other your will?

Why and what will you answer

When those born after us

Will come and ask you about that?

Why, Adama, why?

We were meant to last, still…

Heaven was ours and in wonders we were

Blissful and unaware of all we would no longer share

Water sources were pure and glimmering in the sunshine

Between you and I nothing drew a single wrong line

The Sky used to share the smoothest lights with the Earth

Colourful and rejoicing, they offered us all we deserved

And I used to think, you would always be mine!

Yesssssssss, Heaven was ours and in wonder we were

Blissful and unaware of all we would no longer share

From twilights to dawns and from dawns to twilights

In bliss we swam, living the best of dreams

Eyes wide opened, falling into wonders with no whims

Blessing Life and dancing in harmony throughout sweet lights

Hearts and souls free from vain envy and sorrowful lies

Bodies and spirits out of frustrating and vile desires

Just together, not "inconciliable" like water and fire!

Heaven was ours and in wonders we were

Blissful and unaware of all we would no longer share

[R]

The disillusion and the fall

Alone with the unbearable and sorrowful reality

Dead zone inside out, still I have to face cruelty

In the name of all I once held for true with no vanity

With no sinful desire, and far away from false amenities

The sunlight is now too crude to be faced

Birds' songs sound too sweet to be heard

And the chanting springs and falls now fear

The gloomy thoughts I have now embraced

In the hours through which desolation

Resounds into a very dreadful isolation

In echo with the great disillusion

Signing the cruel and great fall

Into which I am now lost

Here's the time of the fall

Disillusion is yelling, yelling and yelling

And nothing else is to be wished now at
all

If you were to probe my pain

Don't just stand above white plains

Searching for rights and wrongs

Throughout the nights of the strong

No, leave behind all they said is true

Dive all your senses in the deepest waves

And explore the primary ocean's caves

Yes, go beyond the reason of their
reasons,

Far away from the glittering lies they fashion

Every time, everywhere, in all seasons

To fool the world, while waving treason,

As they are veiling the truth as a threat

They just can't allow themselves to share!

Never call my name again,

(since my name in thy mouth is, from now and on, only pure sacrilege)

My name in your mouth

Is now with no doubt

Undeserved and such a shame

Never call my name again

Since you've betrayed me in vain

Now, far away from your presence

I shall breathe again and call for decency

See, even the wind blew away your arrogance

And, of your pretentions and false affection,

None is left to really call for my attention

So don't you call my name again in vain

Since you've asked for my fall and pain

Never call my name again

I've already escaped from your chains

And nothing else shall lit the flame

We once shared in innocence name

Carefully pen your ears and hear this

Since your heart is locked to all of me

And only lies and hatred now remains

Where we used to live and kiss in full bliss!

Never, ever call my name again

Your decision I now abide

After a long run and a breathless ride

And my answer to thee

Is this and shall always be

Never call my name in vain

Cause my name in thy mouth

Is from now and on only pure sacrilege

For both of us in this lost heaven,

Cause' you've lost that old privilege!

God is God

God is God

God is good

God, the most than merciful

God is God

God is good

Do not insult His name in vain anymore

With your insane words

Do not mention His name anymore

To justify all the blood unnecessarily
shed

And to opportunely sign your vain
outrages

For God is not in none of your vile works

God is God

God is great

God, the more than holy One

The highest One, truly,

Blessed be His Name

Always and again

Despite all the false sermons

With which they keep feeding so many
souls,

Who keep drinking at their wells, days
and nights,

The blasphemers, those such beautiful
demons

Always turning people away from the
Lord's holy love!

God is God

God is good

The more than holy One

The Very High One

Blessed be His Name

Always and again

From the soft twilight to the full dawn

No matter the agitation of these great
felons!

Heaven is great

In bliss we are

Bless me in the name of Life

In sunshine we stand and rise

With all that sings and praises

The greatest gift ever chased

For heaven is great

In bliss we rest

With love we pray

Bless me in the sweetness of the sunset

Watch me dancing from dawn to night

And do not ask me why

For in bliss, we are

Yes, in the greatest joy we fall

No matter the names we are called

Bless me at noon

Bless me with the moon

Spreading its smooth light around

For we are those to be found

No matter how long it we'll take

To fly away from all that is fake!

In my purple sunny sky

Day after day, night after night
We fly, we sing and dance

So free and blissful, it's alright

Tasting this great luck

By which we have no left chains

Biding us to all that is vile and vain

In my purple sunny sky

All is wonderful and wild

Here, there is no need to fight

Only wonders, everywhere, at sight

Time is more than an asset

Eternity is ours for the rules we've set

Allowing us to only rejoice

And freely move in love and laugh

No matter what we've been taught

No matter who we are and what we have

From the beginning of time, till now

So, we're happy, at last!

In my purple sunny sky

All is wonderful and wild

Here, there is no need to fight

Only wonders, everywhere, at sight

Come on, join us, if you can

And just do not ask where nor why

We are just free from all that is sad.

Lilith, falling skies

Every shining star in the highest sky

Like a fascinating diamond

In the vast firmament

Still shines in recognition of Lilith,

The first woman, the beautiful Phoenix

Whose rebirth surpasses all myths.

The stars illuminate us with their soft light

To remind us not to fall into the trap

Of these false truths that still feed humanity

Because the spirit often remains prisoner of the mirific prism

Of the pseudo certainties that impose on us so many low attitudes,

Spreading the reflections of all the " isms " forever and again,

From catechism to fanaticism and to fatalism!

The stars sparkle with thousands and thousands of fires

And together, they all proclaim this terrible confession:

No one will never probe the depth of distress

That made Lilith shudder. Lilith,

The one that the untrue writers

Name in their false prayers

"The queen of depravity, so sovereign in evil,

The infamous treacherous! "

No one will ever know that the first tear of the first woman

Shivered the heart of the universe, without ever touching the ground,

Since we have collected and transformed it

So that it will always stay pure and sublime

And by us, ever since, it shines

With thousands and thousands of fires

Always and again chanting that

Lilith is more than want to confess

These despicable and cruel desecrators

Who confined her to the terrible yokes of the underworld

So that, she would never again, break the invisible chains

By which they hold the world, thanks to the great lie,

The one with which they wanted to silence her.

The stars, the eternal witnesses of the original and pure truth

Are still silently speaking about what is ruining our humanity

And they never veil this truth under no canvas

Under their falling skies!

~ Fin ~

Notes

"Then the LORD God called a deep sleep to fall on the man, who fell asleep; he took one of his ribs, and closed the flesh in its place. The LORD God formed a woman from a rib that he had taken from the man, and brought her to the man. And the man then said: « This one is the bone of my bones and the flesh of my flesh! She will be called woman, because she was taken from a part of me, »..., Genesis II, (21-23)

…But as for the fruit of the tree that is in the midst of the garden, God said, you shall not eat of it … out of the tree that is in the midst of the garden, God said, you shall not eat it, neither touch it … ", (Genesis 3: 3).